AF409797

# THE POWER OF HABITS

**7 steps** proven to create the life you want through small actions

Daniel J. Martin

ISBN 978-9916-9938-1-1

Disclaimer: This book has been created with the intention of providing information, suggestions, and guidance on various areas of life, including emotional well-being, mental health, personal growth, and the development of healthy relationships. However, it does not substitute for professional medical care or the advice of a qualified psychologist or therapist. If you are facing serious mental or emotional health issues, we recommend you seek professional help immediately.

*"We are what we repeatedly do. Excellence, then, is not an act, but a habit."*


— Aristotle

# CONTENTS

# DOWNLOAD THE AUDIOBOOK FREE!

*If you would rather enjoy **The power of habits** on the go, **you can download its audio version completely FREE!***

*www.danieljmartin.es/audio/poh*

## INTRODUCTION

# Understanding habits

Everyone has habits. Good or bad, we all operate through routines pre-installed on our hard drives. Our brains. Habits make us who we are. But to what extent are we the owners of our habits? Can we change them? Is it too late to do so?

If you've ever asked yourself a question like this, if you see the years going by and success still eludes you, if you end up abandoning every project you start, if you've become your own Plan B (or C, D, E...Z!), if you're unhappy with the person you are... **This book is for you**.

Because yes, we are the owners of our habits. Yes, we can change them. And no, it's not too late to do it.

Through my work, my research, and – above all – my experience helping my patients, I can assure you that the devil you know is not, in fact, better. The devil you know is reducing your potential. He's getting you accustomed to resignation and a victim mentality. Don't take it! If you're aware of the gap between who you are and who you would like to be, if you feel ashamed of the person you've become, if the success of others feels like a gut punch to you... It's time to take control of your life.

## In the company of your life, your habits are your employees

Before getting started, let's do a quick visualization exercise. Imagine you're the CEO of an important company: your life. As such, you need to analyze and decide which employees to hire and which you're better off without. If these employees were habits, which would you stick with? For example, would you hire Punctuality? What about Proactivity and Efficiency? I bet you would. What about Untidiness? Laziness? Midweek Drinking?

We all know which habits are good for us and which are not. It doesn't take a genius to understand that alcohol is a potential enemy, that our negative thoughts are counterproductive or that junk food is tremendously harmful to our health. But, for one reason or another, we find it so hard to kick these bad habits out of our lives.

## Resistance to change

I'm not telling you anything new when I tell you that **you need to change.** You already know that. That's why you're reading this book. But, as I'm sure you also know, change doesn't come easy. If it did, if we knew how to do it, we wouldn't have hundreds of psychology, neurology and psychiatry studies on why we do the things we do and the things we shouldn't do – nor would therapists' offices be booked up with people frustrated at not reaching their goals.

Resistance makes sense according to our most primal survival instinct: if we've survived so far, why risk changing? What if we fail?

But the truth is that **the only failure is the failure to try**.

Let me suggest a simple exercise:

1. Take a pen and paper and write down everything you did last Monday, in order, from getting up in the morning to going to bed. Do the same for Tuesday. You can do it for the whole week.

Does anything catch your eye?

Did you go to the gym after work like you promised yourself you would? Did you go to the bar too often? Did you make time to read or educate yourself on that subject that you know could mean a career opportunity for you?

Where do you think your current daily routine will take you? Is that the place you dreamed of?

2. Now, let's look at the whys. Why did you spend so many hours in front of the screen on Thursday? Why do you punish yourself by eating junk? Why have you gone to bed late every day?

Got the whys? Now read them.

Most of my patients, when they finish writing their whys and we go over them together, realize that those reasons are actually just excuses.

There are only two whys that keep us anchored to our bad habits and stop us from moving forward to become the people we want to be, and they are: "because I am afraid of change" and "because I don't know how to do it".

If you want to develop new habits that help you build the life you dream of, you need first to eliminate your fear of change, and second to find a method that shows you how to do it.

Over the course of this book, I'll guide you through 7 simple and proven steps to leaving your fears behind and developing any habit you want, effortlessly.

Because habits aren't about getting something, they're about *becoming* someone. So the question is: **who do you want to be?**

Daniel

# Find your why

*"The only way to do great work is to love what you do."*

— Steve Jobs

If you're like most of us mortals, then at some point you will have made the famous list of New Year's resolutions. You know: save money, spend more time with family, eat healthy, read more... Did the list work for you? Did you reach the goals you set yourself?

Generally speaking, no one fulfils the aims they set themselves at the beginning of the year. In fact, statistics tell us 80% of people have already abandoned their resolutions by March, and I'd wager that by October most don't even remember what the resolutions were.

Why does this happen?

There are several reasons. It tends to be the case that we set ourselves **too many goals** at once and that, in addition, they're not accompanied by **a strategy.** For example, the resolution "save money" is doomed to fail if we don't specify: What are our fixed costs? Where can we cut back? How much money are we going to save? Will we save a little each month or do it at specific times? And so on.

You also often find fanciful or **ambiguous goals**, especially after Christmas, along the lines of: "worry less about work" or "enjoy life more". These resolutions are certain to vanish as soon as there's a setback, since they're not aims but rather wishes (it's great to have wishes and fantasies about winning the lottery or sailing across the ocean, but you need to understand the difference between a goal and an "I wish").

Other times, despite a clear aim and a well-designed plan, people **give up without knowing why.** That, sadly, does not only occur with New Year's resolutions. I recall the case of one patient, Adrian, who needed to lose weight and couldn't do it. We had worked on the reasons (the whys) and a gradual workout and diet plan (alongside a nutritionist and a personal trainer). All in vain. However much he tormented himself with the threat of future health problems, and visualized himself looking much better after slimming down, he just kept giving up.

What was wrong with Adrian? Simply put, he hadn't found a real why. Regardless of the many benefits of losing weight, they weren't enough for him to change his habits permanently. Adrian needed **a deeper reason** to commit to real change. I realized that the reason had to do with his **self-image**, with who he was, and not with how much his doctor said he should weigh. And Adrian, among other things, was an attentive and loving father. There, we found his why: Adrian wanted his son to be proud of him, and he hoped to spend a lot of quality time with his son, which meant he needed to take care of his health.

Once we found his why, Adrian felt ready to change, and everything worked out perfectly.

Not all whys are valid for everyone. If someone wants to lose weight, they need to find their own reason for doing it. It doesn't matter if it's an unconventional reason or even a childish one; if that person can relate to it, it will work.

Going back to the Steve Jobs quote from that beginning of this chapter ("The only way to do great work is to love what you do"), we can see that Adrian definitely did NOT love dieting or working out, but he DID love his son. That love drove him to accept the sacrifices he would have to make, and in time, he came to like not only the goal, but also the journey.

## Life purposes

Our true whys relate to our life purposes. A life purpose is the reason or reasons why we get up in the morning, the **deep motivations** that give us a sense of identity and direct our very existence. Life purposes are also the moral guide for our actions, decisions and sacrifices. To live without a purpose is to drift aimlessly.

Jewish neurologist and psychiatrist Viktor Frankl, the author of *Man's Search for Meaning*, studied life purposes in great depth. In his book, considered one of the ten most influential books in the US, expressed many of his experiences of being held captive in concentration camps between 1942 and 1945. There, he sadly bore witness to the total degradation of human beings, and in his absolute despair, he realized something: the prisoners who maintained their will to live despite the calamities they were facing were those who had a reason why. Those who felt that they had unfinished business. That could have been reuniting with a familiar member, setting foot back inside their houses, finish a job they were doing or being able to do something they loved again. The author himself, who lost his pregnant wife in the camps, stated that he would not have survived if not for his determination to write a book. Remember the words of Nietzsche: "He who has a why to live for can bear almost any how".

This may all sound too extreme or philosophical to you: after all, maybe you don't need to review your whole existence just to drop a few pounds. However, as we've said, the real reason why we struggle is not about external factors, but rather our inner selves. And that self must know what it wants and why.

# What is your why?

It's time to find your why. If you truly want to make a change in your life, if you want to achieve new things, you need to know what you're doing it for. Being a good parent, writing a novel, keeping the family business going, passing a test, overcoming anxiety… Everything you aim to do requires sacrifice. **The bigger the sacrifice, the more potent the why needs to be.**

I'm not saying that your why necessarily needs to be epic or capable of changing the course of humanity. It just needs to be important enough to keep you going through battle.

Let's suppose you want to change jobs. My first question would be: "why?". And your answer would probably be one of the following:

- I want to make more money.
- I want more responsibility.
- I want to change sector.

- I want a new environment.
- I want something nearer home.
- ...

In truth, these don't answer my question. These are the things you want to change. They're the *whats*: higher pay, a promotion, a different company, a new sector. But I'm asking you why you want those things. Why do you want more money? Why don't you want to keep doing what you're doing?

When I have this conversation with my patients, we discover that they hadn't gotten to the root of the problem. And it's not until the third round of whys that the real reasons start to come out: "because I don't identify with what I do", "because I'm ashamed of not having been more ambitious", and so on.

Some whys, as you can tell, bring up old conflicts.

If you're not sure as to your why, the following questions might help you:

- Does what you want to achieve work for you? Does it align with your most profound way of being? Or is it something you "should" do because it's expected of you?

- If you eliminated that goal from your life, do you think you would regret it in twenty years' time? (I remember the pain from a woman I treated for depression who told me: "I'll always regret having quit my dance career").

- When you achieve your aim, who will be the first person you tell, and why them?

- If someone could simply bestow that goal upon you tomorrow, would you still want it? Or would you feel like you were cheating? For example, if your goal was to work hard, buy a house and make it a home, would you feel the same satisfaction if the house was gifted to you? If the answer is yes, that's okay (there's nothing wrong with making the most of a stroke of luck), but it means the why for that goal is failing, since you only want to have the house, *not to become that person who works to get the house.*

If you've already found your why, I invite you to write a sentence about it. The sentence should begin with "I want" and be in the present tense.

For example, this is the sentence Adrian wrote when he found his why:

*"I want to diet and work out because that shows through action that I love my son and I make a very big effort to become the father he deserves."*

Got your sentence? Well done. It's a very important step, because it will become your flagship.

Keep your whys to hand – stick them somewhere visible if you need to. Go back to them and to your flagship sentences often, especially when the going gets tough.

# Chapter summary

- We often abandon our goals because we don't have a **real reason** to pursue them.

- Other people's whys **may not be useful** to us.

- **Life purposes** are the compasses guiding our actions and decisions.

- Your why does not need to be epic or admirable to others; you just need to **identify** with it.

- Your **true why** tends to appear after a few rounds of questions regarding why you want to change.

STEP 2

# Draw up your infallible plan

*"The whole world steps aside for the man who knows where is going."*

— Antoine de Saint Exupéry

Once you're clear on why you want to change and you're 100% committed to your cause...it's still possible to fail.

Are you kidding?

No – not if you don't have an effective plan. You need a roadmap so you don't get lost along the way.

How will having a plan help you?

- To get an overall view of your long-term objectives.

- To calculate how long it will take, or, if these are permanent changes, in how much time you can expect to implement them.

- To detect faults or unrealistic perspectives in your aspirations.

- To safeguard your aims against discouragement, self-sabotage and fear.

- As a tool for measuring your progress.

Let's go back to the example of changing jobs: what aspects of your job would you change, and what wouldn't you? Would you accept moving to a sector you like more but where you earn less? What are you hoping for from your new job?

Your plan should go from being general to being as specific as possible. For example, if your change is work-related, you need to know:

1. Exactly what you want to change (for example, wanting to change companies but not job type).

2. Real expectations from that change (like better promotion opportunities, but not necessarily better pay at the start).

3. What you need to do it (training, a project, a team...?).

4. How, when and where you're going to do it.

5. The steps, one by one, in the short, medium and long term.

## Outlining your plan

You've come to the conclusion that you want to change sector. The most efficient way to achieve this is by studying for a master's to get trained up before heading out to look for work. That master's involves two things: saving money each month to pay for it, and finding time to study. It's felt like centuries since you could do either of those things.

Let's begin with the time issue. What are your regular activities and timetables? How much time do you spend working, traveling, working out, relaxing, doing household chores or being with your family? If each week has 168 hours and the master's takes more than 10 hours a week for the next 18 months, what pieces on the board are you going to move around?

Some valid options:

- Getting up earlier.
- Going to bed later.
- Eliminating leisure activities.
- Hiring an agency to clean your home (that will affect your finances).

- Buying ready-prepared food so you don't have to cook or grocery shop (as above).
- Reducing your lunch hour at work so you can leave earlier.
- Dedicating Saturday and Sunday afternoons to your master's.
- And so on.

If this creates tension with your partner or family, how can you make up for that?

Let's continue with other practical aspects: if it's a distance learning program, where are you going to study? Do you have a specific space or will you have to make room on the dinner table, where you eat and fold laundry? (It's not that you can't use that table, but you need to be aware that it has other uses. On top, your books, laptop, notes and other stuff doesn't just float in the air: you will have to put them somewhere accessible where it's not a mission to bring them back to your study area.)

Many of my patients who decide to study having not done so for years find that they're out of the habit. They find it hard to pay attention while reading, summarize, learn new concepts... It doesn't take long for them to get frustrated and start doubting themselves: they think their brain isn't what it was, when what's really failing is their study plan. That's why it's important for your plan to account for some adaptation time to your new habit, as well as strategies for combating self-sabotage and procrastination. What will you tell yourself when you don't get good results on the first try? Or when something "important" happens that you weren't counting on? Or when you find out that someone got the job of your dreams without having a master's?

The more things you can predict beforehand, the more resistant your plan will be to future obstacles.

# Procrastination and last-minute glory

Every day, we're bombarded with last-minute offers and "last call"-type commercials. The last at these prices! Last spots remaining! Last few tickets! It's like how action movie heroes manage to deactivate the bomb at the last second, or rom-com characters don't realize they love each other until the end of the movie, when one of them has to run out the door to stop the other one from catching a plane. Many students brag about cramming for a test the night before, so it seems like everything we achieve at the last minute is worth more and is more authentic than things achieved with calm planning. Without a doubt, that might work in the movies, but it's not for everyday life.

**Procrastination** is the action or habit of putting off tasks you should be seeing to first, substituting them for other activities that are less relevant or more fun. If you have the tendency to procrastinate and have found more than once that you've been saved by the bell, this will have reinforced your bad habit of putting things off.

In reality, procrastination is a waste of time and energy, in addition to subjecting you to a rollercoaster of emotions: you go up with the false satisfaction of "cheating time" when you put your task off, moving into nervousness when you sense that you're running out of time, and then into guilt, anxiety and shame when you're desperately battling the clock, before the final euphoria if you manage to do it in time.

Procrastination is mentally exhausting and creates a feedback loop: the more tired you are, the more tempted you are to leave things to the last minute, which stresses you out and tires you further. Every minute of "pleasure" you get from procrastinating is paid for with many more minutes of stress.

On the other hand, procrastination indicates a low level of commitment: it's like saying, deep down, you don't mind doing things by halves or doing them badly instead of doing them well. But why would you prefer to do things badly?

The answer lies in a hidden part of our brains. There is a voice in there congratulating us on doing things less well than we could have done. It's like a sense of superiority or rebellion. We don't do the grocery shopping when we need to, because we're *more important* than that. We're not like other people.

Have you ever felt that way?

Boring obligations, especially household chores or tasks that everybody has to do and which therefore make us feel less than special, are the perfect targets for procrastination. Because, I mean, what great entrepreneur or genius wastes time on things as frivolous as having clean socks every morning?

But remember: you're not the laundry, or the washer, or the mountain of paperwork you had to prepare to enroll on your master's. You are your habits, and your habits are being a clean and responsible person.

At the other extreme, procrastination can also occur when we spend too much time on the preparation for a given task. Need to send emails to new clients? No problem, first I'll just clean my computer screen, it's dirty. Actually, I'd better just clean my whole desk while I'm at it. Wait, I'm going to sweep the floor, too. Oh, and I have to call the courier company. What time is it? Too late to send emails now. I'll just do it tomorrow.

Does this loop sound familiar to you? When you catch yourself thinking these kinds of things, break the cycle and get to work without listening to your brain: procrastination is holding it hostage.

# Fear of success

Sometimes, procrastination can hide a surprising fear: the fear of success.

We know that fear is apprehension that the new and unknown will bring us unfavorable results. Our primitive brains have been training to survive for thousands of years, which means a strict anti-change policy whenever things are going remotely well. We understand this survival logic when it comes to protecting us from failure, but...what about success?

Whenever we improve in any area, imposter syndrome often crops up. This syndrome involves a fear of being called a fraud or liar by we don't believe in our own worth. As a defense mechanism, our brains anticipate making us feel unworthy of what we have achieved in order to protect us from something worse: the pain or shame of being "found out" or rejected for occupying a place we ultimately don't *deserve*.

Imposter syndrome is a false belief linked to low self-esteem: we don't believe we're worth it or that we deserve for others to trust in the work we're doing (not just in the professional realm, but also in our relationships). In order to free ourselves of this syndrome, we need to work on our self-esteem and demonstrate, in any small way, that we are good at that thing and that we're worthy of others' confidence.

Along with imposter syndrome, there is a fear of being abandoned by our group if our growth generates jealousy or envy. Unfortunately, there is something behind this fear: in fact, it's likely that improving yourself will cause a stir in your friendship group, family or relationship. However, and you should be very clear on this, that should not be your problem. Don't waste time on trying to convince anyone that, despite your personal or professional growth, you're still worthy of their love or trust: those who care about you will still be by your side, and those who don't won't stay there no matter how many times you lend them a hand at your own expense.

## Planning versus "freedom"

Some people criticize habit plans because they believe that an excessively planned life is unexciting and stifles spontaneity. Many of my patients say it to me at the start of their process: "I'm going to be living like a robot!"

But a good habit plan will allow you to optimize your time, money, work capacity and relationships in the long term. Viewed in that way, it gets us closer to freedom, since it affords you more resources to make decisions freely. Without habits, that false sense of "freedom" will soon become aimless wandering.

## Your plan

My advice is for you to spend some real time drawing up your plan and writing it down, using notes, colors or whatever you need to make it easy to understand. You can use a journal, agenda, whiteboard, Post-It notes or any other format that feels effective to you.

What should your plan include?

1. What you've decided to improve on in the form of concrete aims or SMART[1] objectives (you can't just write "lose weight"; you need to be specific).

2. Everything you're going to do in order to achieve it: new habits, schedules, dates, changes in your spending dynamic, improvements in self-care, and so on.

3. Possible obstacles (and their solutions, if you know them. You can note these down as and when you encounter them).

4. What to give up: the things you'll have to forego for the duration of the plan or permanently.

---

[1] Explained in depth in *The power of self-confidence*.

5. All the answers to all the questions you can foresee right now.

It's important to be specific. If you've decided to get in shape, make it clear that you will go to the gym on Tuesdays and Thursdays at *x* time, to *x* class, for the next *x* months, and the milestones you're committed to reaching. If you want to work out to participate in a race in the future, write down the name and date of the race and research a realistic training plan, with short- and long-term goals.

Don't hesitate to seek advice when drawing up your plan. There are tons of professionals who can help you:

- Life coaches.
- Psychologists.
- Personal trainers.
- Nutritionists.
- Financial advisors.
- Image consultants.

- Private tutors in any subject.
- Etc.

Keep in mind the things you're going to be giving up. It's not a bad idea to write them down as if they were lines at school. These are some examples taken from my sessions:

- I can't stay more than a half hour on the couch after dinner.

- I can't go on vacation this year.

- From now on, my leisure budget for the weekends will be $x$.

- I will get rid of (sell) two of my guitars to pay for music lessons.

- I can't eat more than 1 bakery item per week.

# A second opinion

Show your plan to someone you trust and ask them what they think. Two notes on this: the first, if you're going to "use" friends or relatives to help you in your growth, don't forget to thank them and do something in return when they ask. Everyone likes to help, but nobody likes to feel used.

The second is a tip on "trusted" people: we've already talked about people who will be envious when they see you grow and who will want you to fall. But there are also people who won't be able to help you no matter how much they'd like to. I mean, maybe your grandmother is not the best person to review your plan (with all the love in the world for my dear grandmas). However much they want the best for you, they probably won't be able to understand your plan or give you suitable feedback. In this case, a trusted person would be someone with experience in the aims and habits you're looking to work on.

It's important that you don't move onto the next chapter until you've written up your plan. When you've done it, we will look at methods for etching those new habits onto your mind and kicking useless or toxic routines. Both those things will be based on this plan, so what you've written in it counts.

# Chapter summary

- Drawing up a plan for your new aims will help you to optimize your time and battle against your own resistance to change.

- Your plan should include what you're going to do in the most specific way possible and detail all possible problems.

- Your plan should also consider the sacrifices you will have to make and things you'll have to give up.

- The more foolproofed a plan is, the lower the risk you will procrastinate or abandon it.

- Procrastination is simply fear – of success or failure – and a lack of respect towards ourselves.

- Not only will your plan lead you to a healthier and more productive life; it will also bring you peace and self-confidence.

# Your new habits

*"First we form habits, then they form us."*
— Rob Gilbert

We have the why, we have the what, now let's look at the how.

We're going to put into practice what's in your plan. Unlike the previous aspects, the how is a very mechanical part: it's about executing and repeating the actions we have planned until we reach our goal.

It may seem exhausting at first, but once the wheel starts turning, everything will get easier.

Let's imagine you've made the following two decisions: from Monday to Friday, you will get up and go to bed a half hour earlier. How are you going to get yourself used to this?

Charles Duhigg, winner of a Pulitzer Prize for his research into corporate habits, states that any individual or collective habit, however long we've had it, can be changed or introduced if we understand how our brains work.

As we've said, everyone has habits. Habits are defined as the set of repeated and internalized actions we carry out automatically without needing to think about them. Habits help us in our daily lives, giving known answers to most contexts: this simplifies our lives, freeing our brains from routine tasks in order to concentrate on things that require our attention.

However, each of those routine actions is the result of an initial, conscious decision that then became a habit. That action had an optimal or favorable result (reward), so we did the same thing again when in that situation. Our brains learned that that was the way to do things, and the action became a habit.

Every habit has three consecutive phases. Duhigg calls these **cue, routine** and **reward**.

The **cue** is the external trigger that puts us into a situation and asks us for a response or routine. The cue always comes from outside, from our environments. For example: the traffic light turned green (cue) > I see that and start moving the car (response or routine).

To know the degree to which we have internalized a cue, we can try doing the opposite to what we usually do when that cue appears. Let's imagine the meanings of red and green were reversed on traffic lights: how hard would we find it to get accustomed to the new situation? We'd probably mess up more than once. We experience something similar when we go abroad to a country where they drive on the left: I guarantee you that even the most experienced driver becomes a nervous, clumsy beginner when they have to start driving on the opposite side from what they're used to.

The **routine** is the somewhat automatic action we undertake once we have received the cue: the light turns green and you press down on the gas, get home and take your shoes off, a WhatsApp notification goes off and you look at your phone, and so on.

The **reward** is what we get for that action, and it can be something as basic as knowing that we followed the rules and didn't get in an accident. The reward is not random or new: it's exactly what we expect to happen every time we react to a cue in a certain way.

This whole ritual happens and we barely even notice it.

So, if our habits are automatic, how can we change them at this point?

## How to introduce a new habit

Now, let's go back to our change in schedule. Going to sleep a half hour earlier shouldn't be an issue, but for years you've spent an hour in front of the TV after dinner. It's your time to relax, talk to your partner or interact with social media. The first day that you cut that in half, you feel like something's missing. It's as if a really nice little chunk of your day has been stolen from you. On top of that, you don't go to sleep any earlier, so you really didn't gain anything.

However, you know that gaining that half hour is important. What can you do?

First, identify the different parts of the habit: the cue, routine and reward.

1. The cue: what exactly is it that begins that ritual? Is it talking about your series over dinner? Is it carrying the dirty dishes to the kitchen once you've eaten? Is it the sound the TV makes when you turn it on?

2. The routine: what do you do during that hour? Do you talk, eat snacks, watch videos on your phone, play Xbox?

3. The reward: What do you feel after the previous point? The pleasure of switching off? Of being on the couch? Of the snacks? All those things at once? If you're not sure, eliminate each of those options in turn while maintaining the rest of the ritual: one night, try going the whole hour without turning on the TV (or substituting that with anything new), another night, try without your phone, another, without the snacks, and so on. What is it exactly that you find comforting?

4. Once you're clear on that, you need to find a way to make up for what you've sacrificed. One

way to do this is to find an alternative reward that's as close to what you have now as possible:

- If it's about watching a series, try finding a series with shorter episodes.

- If it's feeling yourself gradually getting sleepier, try listening to a relaxation podcast in bed to help speed up the process.

- If it's chatting with your partner, try calling them on the way home from work.

That way, you're not eliminating the habit – you're just modifying it in your favor.

## Clear's Four Laws theory

James Clear is another great expert in the creation of habits. Based on the work of Charles Duhigg, Clear developed his own theory on habits based on four laws or basic conditions. Let's take a look at them.

As we said above, what triggers the start of a habit is the cue. Once the cue is received, according to Duhigg, we give our response – but for Clear, there is a step in between: **craving**. The craving appears when we perceive the cue and automatically anticipate the reward: you hear the sound of the TV turning on (cue) > you want to eat chocolate (craving) > you eat the chocolate (routine) > you feel good (reward).

The difference between this four-part pattern (cue – craving – routine – reward) and that of Duhigg lies in the preprogrammed craving: if another person performed the ritual but had never eaten chocolate at that time, they wouldn't think about the chocolate upon receiving the cue because they wouldn't have created that association. In other words, the craving would not appear and they would probably not eat chocolate.

According to Clear, in order for a ritual to become a habit, each of the parts must comply with one condition: the cue must be obvious, the craving attractive, the response easy to do and the reward satisfying.

So, what do we need to do to introduce a new habit? We need to ensure that it meets the above four conditions:

- CUE – It must be obvious and identifiable: 1st condition or law.
- CRAVING – It must be attractive and anticipate the reward: 2nd condition or law.
- ROUTINE – It must be easy to perform once learned: 3rd condition or law.
- REWARD - It must be satisfying and meet the expectations of the craving: 4th condition or law.

Let's imagine you have been prescribed a medicine for the next two months. You need to take a pill every morning. When you get home, you leave the pills in the medicine cabinet and, of course, the next morning you forget to take the pill.

You need to create a habit to make taking the pill part of your life. In this case, it might be sufficient to leave a note or put the box of pills next to the coffee machine. This way, the routine of taking the pill becomes easier and more pleasant, since it comes before breakfast.

## Tricks and resources

As you can tell, you often have to use your imagination to strengthen new habits. Below, I share with you some of the tactics my patients use, many of which are the fruit of their own processes of trial and error:

- Strategic placement of objects: your gym bag by the front door, your book on your pillow, your water bottle next to your computer, your vegetables already prepared and placed on the most visible shelf in the refrigerator, and so on.

- Sandwich technique: slipping your new habit in between habits you have already internalized (like your morning pill next to the coffee machine).

- Reminders: using alarms, notes, diaries or phone apps to remind you to do things.

- If you're finding a task very tedious and boring, focus on breaking the first-minute barrier: concentrate all your attention and willpower on the act of beginning the routine, as that's the hardest part. (How many times have you heard people say that the hard part is getting started but once you do, it's easy?). That stops you from being overwhelmed thinking about the whole task you have ahead of you (for example, going through all your supplier invoices); all you have to do is open the folder and look at the first invoice.

All these tricks may seem cumbersome, but they're only necessary at the start: once you've developed the habit, your brain will make it much easier on you.

## How to get rid of a bad habit

Think back to the Rob Gilbert quotation at the start of this chapter: "First we form habits, then they form us". That's actually only half of what he said. He went on to say: "Conquer your bad habits or they will conquer you."

We all have bad habits. Eating more than we need to, drinking, impulse buying, neglecting the housework, not resting enough, not controlling our tempers... Those habits tend to be more deep-seated than we believe, and they usually satisfy impulses we can't control. In order to protect them, our brains tell us things like this:

"There's nothing wrong with having a glass of wine when you get home from work."

Of course, there's nothing wrong with it, but...have you tried seeing how you feel if you *don't* have that glass? How frustrated and anxious would you really feel?

"I know I shouldn't buy so many clothes, but I can't help it; I love wearing new things."

Where do you think this impulse comes from?

If you want to kick a bad habit, first you need to be aware of how it works and what it's responding to. What is the reward, and why is it a bad reward?

Our bad habits didn't just appear out of nowhere: at some point in our lives, they fulfilled a purpose that was useful at the time. Perhaps they calmed us down or comforted us in a hostile environment. Or maybe we adopted the habit through simple imitation of our surroundings. That's why, if you have wisely decided that you no longer want them in your life, you can get rid of them without judgment: mentally thank them for their services and announce without hatred or resentment that they can no longer be in your life.

## Bring your bad habits to a rational place

The psychoanalyst Carl G. Jung said: "Until you make the unconscious conscious, it will direct your life and you will call it fate."

We can only change what we are aware of. We can only stop biting our nails if we realize that we are about to do it at the point at which our fingers come up to our mouth. We can only stop interrupting people if we keep our full attention on our impulse to intervene in the conversation.

However automatic a habit has become, it is possible to change or eliminate it if you begin to rationalize it and do it consciously. It is as if you are seeing it for the first time in your life.

Let's take breathing, for example. It's an unconscious habit; we breathe even when we are asleep. But we can learn to *control* our breathing by paying attention to the act of inhaling and exhaling air. If you want to sing, swim or speak in public, for example, that is what you will have to do – and you can only achieve that by practicing the habit of breathing consciously.

## Changing a bad habit by following the four laws of Clear

On a mechanical level, a bad habit works the same as a good one: a cue incites a craving, which we satisfy with a routine in order to obtain a reward. You're in the office, you see two colleagues walking toward the coffee machine, you think about coffee and you automatically stop concentrating on your work because you start to daydream about how nice a cup of coffee would be.

Following this logic, if you want to eliminate or modify a bad habit, you need to find a way to "trick" your brain into losing interest in that habit:

- CUE: make it invisible rather than obvious. For example, avoid being able to see the area where your colleagues walk (perhaps by placing a visual barrier there), or put headphones in so you can't hear your workmates getting out of their chairs.

- CRAVING: make it less appealing rather than irresistible. For example, hit the brakes on your need for coffee with a note reminding you of the time you waste taking those breaks and which you then have to make up later, and another note to remind you how bad the coffee actually is.

- RESPONSE: make it difficult or tedious instead of easy. Don't keep cash around for the machine, go when there are more people so that you have to waste time waiting in line (or go when there's nobody there so that you can't stop for a chat, if that's the part you like), don't put sugar in your coffee, and so on.

- REWARD: make it unsatisfactory instead of gratifying: leave your cup after the first sip, through a dollar in the trash for every coffee you buy, and so on.

Some of these tactics look ridiculous and you would be embarrassed having to explain them. But you would be surprised at the things people will do to kick a bad habit.

## The case of Oliver

Oliver was mad at himself because he couldn't stop drinking during the week. It's not that he drank a lot – just a few beers every day after work. But he was annoyed at not being able to quit it. Every time he tried, he got in a bad mood, found it hard to sleep that night, or had headaches.

We began to analyze his habits beginning from when he received the cue inciting him to drink right up to when he went to bed.

1. The cue was appearing on his way home: from the moment Oliver left work, everything he saw around him – buildings, stores, kids leaving school, and so on – was familiar to him and reminded him that it was *that time*.

2. The craving shot up during that journey: Oliver couldn't wait to get home and have that cold beer, because it marked the end of one

more working day and charged his batteries for the rest of the day.

3. The routine of drinking it was a real ritual: Oliver would loosen his shoes and sit on the couch. It was a moment where he didn't look at his phone or talk to anyone. He would breathe deeply, look out the window or close his eyes: subconsciously, he was doing relaxing things during those few minutes while giving himself the dose of alcohol that his body was crying out for.

4. Finally, the reward was the sensation of having recharged and being ready for action again. Of course, recharging was a positive thing – the mistake was in thinking that it had been the beer that did it (let's not underestimate the manipulative power that alcohol has on our brains...).

We began by masking the cue to make it harder for the craving to kick in. To do this, we tried changing some of the steps that were causing him to think about beer:

- Oliver changed his route home at random so that it wasn't familiar to him and he had to concentrate on getting back.
- Other times, instead of going home, he would go to the park, grocery store or gym.
- Sometimes he would invent mental games or distractions as he made his way home.
- He also began listening to podcasts that kept him focused.
- Right when he got to his building, Oliver would turn up his headphones' volume until it was almost annoying, and kept it at that high level for the first few minutes after getting home.
- Sometimes, he would walk or jog up the stairs rather than using the elevator, so that when he got to his apartment, all he really wanted to do was get his breath back.

Continuously changing the way he went home made the cue less obvious, and the craving was delayed or mixed in with other things that Oliver had to attend to.

To make the craving less appealing, Oliver committed to thinking about the consequences of alcohol addiction any time he thought about beer, or he called to mind some teetotal celebrities he admired.

Then, we put some tactics into practice to make the response more difficult and the reward less pleasurable:

- Stop keeping beer in the house.
- Leave beers outside the refrigerator so that they were warm when he got home.
- Substitute them for alcohol-free beer.
- Leave the kitchen door closed and display some notes with reminders to do other things.

- Place objects on the couch so that he couldn't automatically sit down and would have to spend a few minutes clearing them away.
- Make a phone call to the switchboard of an official institution and focus on the conversation with the machine: something which made Oliver feel nervous.

Many of the tactics didn't work. For example, not keeping beer in the house didn't help Oliver, because he knew there was none and kept stopping by the store to get some on his way home. What he did find was that not being able to sit on the couch was what bugged him most.

Finally, Oliver managed to eradicate the habit by getting hooked on true crime podcasts and switching the beer for a no-alcohol version by the same brand. The rest of the habit remained intact, so the sensation of recharging his batteries and feeling refreshed after a few minutes on the couch continued. All we eliminated was the alcohol.

# Learning from minimalism

It's no secret that we live in a spiral of consumerism in which we essentially work in order to buy.

But it is possible to improve our purchasing habits: in fact, it's one of the greatest tasks that faces us as a society.

Joshua Fields and Ryan Nicodemus are lifelong friends known all over the world for being minimalists. These two ex-CEOs, who made tons of money from their corporate jobs, realized that their buying habits were absolutely insane. So, they got rid of all their belongings that they didn't consider essential and began, along with other people, a movement in favor of conscious consumption.

In my view, the most interesting part of this movement is that it's not some pseudo religion that advocates for a life of suffering in order to find truth, nor is it a trendy challenge, nor is it about the environment (all I mean is that it doesn't urge you to do things for anyone else's sake, just for yourself).

Minimalism argues for the reeducation of our consumer habits in order to have more meaningful lives. It asks us to question how many of the things we buy are necessary or make us happy, and how many of the things we have at home were bought out of obligation and not because they truly make our lives easier[2].

Here are some reflections and tips on rewriting your consumer habits:

1. Before you buy something, wait its price in hours: if it costs fifty dollars, wait fifty hours before you buy it. If it costs a thousand, wait a thousand hours.

---

[2] According to data, the average family home in the US contains around 300,000 objects.

2. Give the three Rs a change: recycle, reuse and reduce.

3. Make shopping lists and stick to them.

4. If something comes into your house, something else has to go.

5. Unsubscribe from any emails to avoid propaganda.

6. Stop "window shopping" online.

7. Sales: would you buy that thing if it were not on sale? Were you thinking about buying one before you saw it?

8. Buy things thinking about yourself, not others. This is as valid for a bag you buy to impress your colleagues as it is for a guitar like the one your favorite guitarist has – who, by the way, is a millionaire.

9. Translate the price of what you want to buy into working hours. How much time do you have to work in order to buy that?

10. Parties, birthdays, celebrations and Christmas: make deals with your family and friends to limit spending, or agree to give

more conscious gifts that aren't just for the sake of it.

11. Vacations and leisure: before booking your next trip to a fashionable location, remember what vacations are for and what you're hoping for from your next getaway.

Although everyone needs to find their own way to handle their money, we have a moral obligation to ourselves not to spend our lives working just to buy things to earn others' respect or calm our anxiety.

"We spend money that we do not have, on things we do not need, to impress people who do not care." — Will Smith

# Chapter summary

- Our habits are rituals that follow a logical sequence: they begin with a cue that triggers our craving for a reward, and we react by performing a certain action in order to get that reward.

- In order for habits to be sustained over time, each of these stages must fulfil a condition: the cue must be obvious, the craving irresistible, the routine easy, and the reward gratifying or comforting.

- When it comes to either introducing or eliminating or modifying a habit, we must follow these four rules.

- We can all use this to improve our habits, even those which don't appear to pose a problem (such as our buying habits).

- Agendas, Post-It notes, reminders and other resources can help you get started.

# Avoid falling back into bad habits

*"Each day is a series of conflicts between the right path and the easy path."*

— Popular saying

Do you remember the introduction to this book, when we were imagining your habits as employees of your company? Remember that we wanted to hire Punctuality and fire Laziness?

Well, there's no doubt that your bad habits will become disgruntled and vengeful employees once you fire them: they were with you for so long that now they feel you owe them something.

That's why they will be knocking at your door, trying to sabotage your company. They will make you feel unsure, threaten you with a "don't come crawling back when the new *me* you're hiring doesn't work out", or take aim at your deepest wounds with phrases like: "you think you're going to win your father's approval by doing this?".

Don't give them the time of day.

Before a relapse, there is always something that destabilizes the process. This can be either external or internal. We've already talked about procrastination and self-sabotage, which are internal, but it can also happen that, for example, someone who hasn't touched a drop in years receives some bad news one day and falls back into alcoholism.

In this chapter, we will look at how to strengthen your willpower and perseverance so you can keep going even when things are stacked against you. Once again, you might find some of these techniques eccentric or ridiculous, but if I've included them in this book it's because they worked for someone not so different from you.

To begin, here are ten things you can do in your everyday life to help train your willpower:

1. Talk to your temptations when they appear. Treat them as if they were an unwanted visitor you need to get rid of quickly but politely: "I'm sorry, but I can't see you right now." "I'm sorry, I don't do this any more."

2. Talk to yourself (nicely) when you feel like giving up and going back to your old habits because *they weren't so bad.* Talk to yourself like you would a good friend, or write yourself a letter. What would you say to yourself if you weren't you?

3. Use anti-anxiety techniques. There are lots of resources, from meditation to therapeutic

writing. Remind yourself that anxiety is just the messenger, and it will go away.

4. Give your word. Find someone who you wouldn't want to disappoint and tell them what you're trying to achieve. Committing your honor and pride will help you to keep going.

5. Put money down. Decide on an amount of money it would hurt to lose, and give it up every time you fail. For example: every time you don't perform a task, you will transfer a hundred dollars to your football team's rivals or donate it to your most hated political party.

6. Mark each successful day on a calendar and put it somewhere you can see it. Little by little, the calendar will fill with small achievements, and breaking your streak will feel increasingly worse.

7. If the task is repetitive and boring, divide it up and intersperse it with fun things, or show

your progress in a quantifiable way. For example, you could use the "bowls of paperclips" technique. Start each day with one bowl of paperclips and another, empty bowl. Every time you complete a task, move one clip from the full bowl to the other, so that you can visualize what you've already done.

8. Remove anything that might be a cue: don't go for lunch at the mall if you know you have trouble controlling your spending, change your journey home to avoid driving past the bar, ask a trusted neighbor to look after your games console for a week, use cellphone apps to block your access to websites you don't want to look at.

9. Avoid making excuses to yourself when you skip a routine.

10. You can skip your habit for one day if it's for a good reason, but never two.

## A Facebook of admirable people

I'm going to propose an activity I often suggest to my patients. It's about creating a "Facebook" (in its literal sense: a book of faces) of people you admire. Those people could be alive now or have lived centuries ago, and they might be business owners, activists, artists, elite sportspeople, scientists or your grandpa who worked down the mines all his life.

The idea is to have a book of photos of all the people who motivate you to keep going. You can find their photos online and print them out next to their name and the battle or characteristic that you admire about them. That way, when you're tempted to give up, you can turn to this "Facebook" to encourage you to keep fighting for your goals.

## Your worst photo

A few years ago, I met an actor who had overcome a terrible cocaine addiction. He told me that one of the things that helped him avoid relapses was a photo of himself. It wasn't a nice photo: a stranger had taken it one morning when the actor had left his home after several days locked up suffering from severe withdrawal syndrome. His appearance was horrifying. The photo went viral and did the rounds on social media. Back then, the actor didn't care at all.

But later on, in a therapy session, I suggested to him that he get ahold of that photo and look at it often, to remind himself: "that's a place I never want to go back to".

I'm sure that, even if not as extreme as that, you have "photos" you wouldn't like to see the light of day. They don't need to be real photos – just picture them in your head. They might be of you lying on the couch at eleven o'clock at night watching the third episode of a series in a row, or you inventing excuses to justify not doing something you promised you would, or you losing your nerve...

When you fail at a task or are tempted to, remembering potentially shameful images of yourself will help you react.

## Choose your hard

This is another technique for strengthening your willpower. Simply choose the option you prefer:

- Dieting and watching what you eat is hard. Dealing with health problems in the future when you can't turn back the clock is hard. Choose your hard.

- Maintaining a relationship is hard. Being alone at the worst and best moments of your life is hard. Choose your hard.

- Having the discipline to practice for an hour every day is hard. Realizing in time that you never learned to play guitar and you only ever talked about it is hard. Choose your hard.

I think you get the picture.

## What to do when nothing changes

Sometimes, we can make a huge effort to better ourselves, only to find that nothing seems to be changing. There are no visible changes in our lives.

You might feel like this at times. Before I respond to this, let me tell you a well-known Japanese fable:

Kishiro was a humble carpenter for whom things were going very badly. He was on the verge of closing his business. One day, in desperation, he went to a wise man to ask for advice.

"Can you give me a reason not to give up?" he begged.

"Look at my garden," replied the wise man. "Do you see the ferns and the bamboo?"

"Yes," replied the carpenter.

"When I planted them, the ferns grew quickly. They quickly carpeted the ground in bright green. But the bamboo seed didn't grow at all. However, I never gave up on the bamboo. I kept on watering the earth where it was planted.

"By the next year, the ferns had grown even brighter and lusher, but the bamboo still had not sprouted. The following two years, the same thing happened. But I never gave up on the bamboo, and I kept watering the earth. After four years of waiting, on the fifth year, a little bamboo shoot poked its way through the soil. The sixth year, the bamboo grew sixty feet tall. It had spent five years putting down roots that could sustain it; that was why it had taken so long to grow."

"How did you know the bamboo would eventually grow, after all those years?"

"I didn't," replied the man. "But I never stopped doing what I had to do. I never gave up on the bamboo."

The bamboo is a good example of what perseverance means: five years go by before the first shoot appears, and then...it turns out to be the fastest-growing plant on the planet!

James Clear talks about perseverance in a similar way in his book *Atomic Habits*. He urges us to improve by just one per cent every day. At the end of each day, we won't notice results. Probably not by the end of each week, either. But if we persevere, by the end of each year, we will be 37% better – and that *will* make a difference.

# Why do I relapse?

So, a few months have gone by and you've abandoned your goals. You've fallen back into your old ways: wasting time in front of screens, giving up on your projects, spending tons of money on things that do nothing for you, or betraying your partner's trust again.

There are only two real reasons why you might interrupt or abandon a good habit. The first is a force majeure event that you couldn't predict and that makes it physically impossible for you to continue: a pandemic, sickness, a terrible misfortune, and so on. The other reason is that your belief in yourself (your self-image) has been blocked or sabotaged. Something inside you is telling you you're not *that person*.

Let's go back to Adrian's example.

Before he found a real reason to take better care of himself, Adrian kept on relapsing over and over, because he was focused on his goal (to lose thirty pounds) and not on who he was ("I'm a father who does things for my son"). One way or another, instead of working from himself and toward his goal (from the inside out: "I'm a good father and take care of myself for my son, so I am losing thirty pounds"), Adrian was working from his goal toward himself ("I need to drop thirty pounds in order to be valid").

In his theory on habits, James Clear describes the inside/out dynamic and explains why the biggest changes in habits – those that require great and sustained effort – need to be worked on from the inside out: in other words, not by waiting for our results to validate us, but rather by understanding that we are *that person* who is capable and who wants to reach those results. The dynamic, then, goes from our identity (who we are) toward our goals:

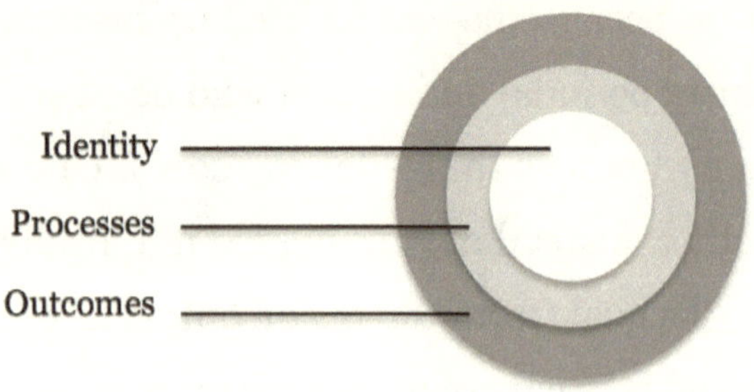


Let's say you want to be a writer. That's your goal. But what does it mean to be a writer? Is it publishing a novel? Writing a bestseller? Making a living from your writing?

In reality, it's much more obvious: a writer is someone who writes. In other words, it's someone who spends hours and hours on the act of writing. Publishing a novel, winning a prestigious award or getting on a bestsellers list are just a few of the somewhat probably results of becoming a writer.

If your goal is to be a writer, and being a writer means writing, how do you become a writer?

Well, by spending hours writing. Because – and here comes the interesting part of all these obvious statements – when you write, *you become a writer*. Every time Adrian went to the gym or stuck to his weekly meal plans, *he was reaffirming the good and responsible father that he knew he was.*

No matter how good our habits our, we can't achieve our goals if our self-concept tells us we are "not that kind of person". When Adrian tried to lose weight because he thought it was what he had to do or because the doctors were telling him to, he quickly became demotivated and gave up. Something within him was sabotaging the "new" him. In contrast, when Adrian associated the "new" him with an aspect of his identity that he did believe in ("I'm a good father"), things changed.

Let's look at another example.

Rosa is a young woman with attention deficit disorder whom I helped some time ago. She lived alone and, among other things, her disorder caused her to be incredible messy at home. Not only did she lose things and constantly forget what she had in the refrigerator, but her house was always a bombsite.

We could say that Rosa *was* untidy, given that most of the time, her house was a total mess. Only once a week, usually on Sundays, would Rosa attempt to tidy up.

But Rosa *was* tidy. When I told her that in our first session, she gave me a look: "No, really. I'm untidy. I guess I wouldn't be if I didn't have ADD, but as it happens, I *am* untidy."

"Yes," I told her. "You're untidy most of the time, but you're also tidy on Sundays."

"Right," she said, "but that doesn't count. Being tidy means keeping things in order."

What I wanted to change was Rosa's self-image: I wanted her to go from believing that she was messy to believing that she was untidy when the house was untidy, and tidy when it wasn't. If I could get that idea into her head, Rosa would stop defining herself as an untidy person.

We began with just one thing: her clothes. For the next two weeks, I asked Rosa to focus solely on keeping her clothes clean and tidy, doing laundry every day. That was all. Everything else, including towels and sheets, could look like a tornado had blown through until it came to her cleaning day. I asked her to be aware, every time she did her laundry (and folded it, ironed it, and so on), that she was being tidy at that moment, and to time it.

Then, we added up those time periods and wrote them down on a calendar. Little by little, the calendar filled up with little pockets of time in which Rosa *was* tidy. Two weeks later, we added dishes and cups. I asked her to be aware of it every time she cleared away dishes and cups – that was all. Rosa began to see that the time she spent being tidy was increasing to the point that, one week, she spent more time being tidy than not.

Of course, we used a lot of techniques and resources to reinforce her cleaning habits, such as alarms, notes, strategic placement of objects, prizes, and so on – but it was seeing the time periods during which she was tidy that did away with her belief that she *was* an untidy person.

If you're finding a habit hard to kick, you should stop to think about how it relates to your self-image and what false beliefs you hold about it. Then, you can review the three stages (identity – process – results) to see what direction you're working in.

# Chapter summary

- Perseverance and willpower are skills that can be trained and reinforced with tactics to make performing tasks more agreeable.

- Some activities, such as "Facebook of admirable people", "Your worst photo", and "Choose your hard" may help you when you're tempted to abandon your goals.

- Small progress is still progress: if you improve just 1% every day, by the end of the year, you'll be 37% better.

- If you relapse, check your self-image: maybe you hold a belief that is sabotaging you.

# Surround yourself with the right environment

*"I have turned away from anything that could weaken my willpower, beginning with alcohol, which subjugates so many people."*

— María Félix

We know that motivation is essential for achieving any objective, but so is your environment.

The people you interact with, your workspace, your places of leisure, your family relationships... It all contributes to creating a favorable or unfavorable setting for your interests. It's no coincidence that many people go into similar careers to those of their parents, or that in certain societies or cities there is a tendency towards a particular work culture.

Our habits are linked to our surroundings. The cue itself is given by our environment, and the same environment leads to our response – or routine – being either easy or difficult to perform (the second of Clear's laws). Teenagers who encounter three betting shops on their way to school are more likely to get into gambling than those who see none. People who grow up in families where no one sets an example in terms of effort are likely to seek jobs or relationships that require very little of them.

It's true that some people achieve incredible success despite having been raised in very harmful environments (we all know a few cases like that), but they tend to be the exception: statistics all point to the opposite.

# Group strength

We have already talked about how our groups can have a negative influence: jealousy and peer pressure when one member of a group begins to better themselves ("you're not the person you used to be", "you've forgotten where you come from") can make them doubt their own goals or worth. Don't let that happen.

Of course, things that jeopardize our goals can come from anywhere. Your best friend might annoy you one day for some reason, or the best boss in the world could have a bad morning and decide not to approve a great pitch you make. But an environment that systematically prevents you from growing is a toxic one, and you need to avoid it.

To evaluate this, all you have to do is analyze from time to time the behavior of the groups you belong to. Here are twenty-five red flags you shouldn't ignore, whether at work, in your friendship group, within your family or in your relationship:

1. You feel like your new habits or goals are going to be poorly received.
2. You hide your new habits and projects in order to avoid problems in that environment or group.
3. Your environment forces you to do things that don't sit right with you.
4. You're not sure exactly what's keeping you where you are.
5. There is a leader in that setting to whom you owe a great degree of loyalty.
6. You pay for things you didn't do.
7. You're reluctant to leave that environment for fear of possible recriminations.
8. You have been humiliated more than once.
9. Your surroundings make you nervous rather than relaxing you.
10. There is a lot of unpredictability that keeps you constantly on high alert.
11. Your surroundings exhaust or confuse you.

12. You're constantly moderating your behavior or words.

13. There are annoying comparisons made between members of the group or with people external to the group.

14. You feel like you need permission in order to act.

15. There are internal, almost secret rules that no one outside that environment would understand.

16. When, for whatever reason, your activity within that group temporarily decreases, you feel relieved.

17. You always feel you need to change something. You're never enough for that group just the way you are.

18. You really want to know what life is like *out there*.

19. You don't feel lucky to be in those surroundings – quite the opposite.

20. You feel like your problems are never important to those people.

21. Sometimes you believe that, deep down, your problems are your fault for being the way you are.
22. You sometimes feel that you have been manipulated or lied to.
23. Your surroundings jeopardize other relationships or aspects of your life.
24. You feel like you're either with that group of people, or against them.
25. If you try to leave the environment, everyone blocks you.

This book isn't about toxic relationships, but it's important to be clear that an environment contrary to your interests is going to make life hard for you.

On the other hand, positive surroundings are hugely useful for achieving a goal. Whether it's winning a championship, overcoming trauma or reaching a collective professional goal, it's true what they say: there's strength in numbers. We can all call to mind some case of a sports team that was modest but cohesive and overcame challenges seemingly out of their reach: as well as organizations like Alcoholics Anonymous, where the constant support of others is part of its success.

If you're facing challenges you have no benchmark for, or you believe your environment won't accept your new productive habits, go elsewhere. Find examples and become an example to others, too. There are eight billion people in the world, and nowadays you can connect with people anywhere on the planet. The world is too big for your mental boundary to end where your friend says it should.

One of the most common and obvious examples of group strength when it comes to either reinforcing or undermining your new habits is weight loss. I often "joke" with my patients who want to begin a weight loss journey that the quickest and most effective way to reach their desired weight isn't through a good nutritionist or personal trainer, but by changing their friendship group. And although I'm kidding when I tell them to get new friends overnight, it's really not a joke that it would be the most effective way to do it. Because it's normal for your friends to be similar to you. And if, so far, you've been a sedentary person, you probably hang around with other sedentary people. For better or for worse, you deciding to change your habits won't make your group of friends want to follow the same path as you so you can all support each other. Quite the opposite. Your group is going to want you "the way you are": the way they have always known you. Sedentary.

The good thing about this phenomenon is that it works both ways. So, if you want to maintain your weight loss habits – despite your friends – for as long as possible, it's normal for you to begin to socialize more with more active people who are pursuing the same goals as you or, better yet, have already reached them. And these new people, this new friendship group, will also get rid of you if you start flagging one day and try to go back to your old, sedentary habits. Because they don't want you to change – they want you the way they've always known you, "the way you are": a healthy and active person.

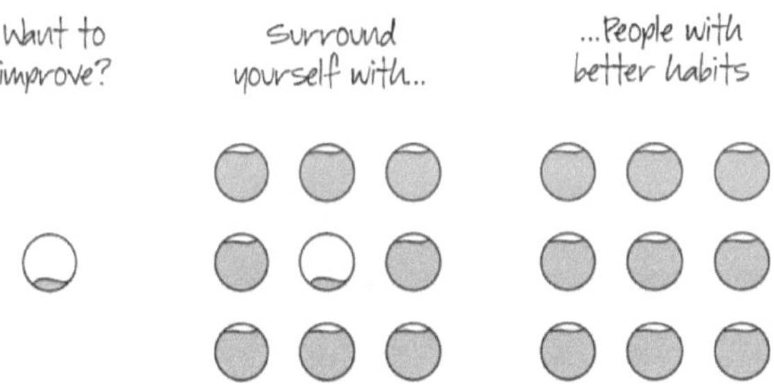


Group strength is truly powerful. It's up to you whether you let it hold you back or you use it to your favor.

## Order can make or break you

By this point, we all know or should know the Japanese entrepreneur and consultant Marie

Kondo. This advocate of orderly spaces developed an entire philosophy concerning the habit of keeping our homes clean and tidy, since this has a positive impact on our health and emotional wellbeing.

In alignment with minimalists, Marie Kondo argues for only keeping in your home objects that are necessary or that make you happy. She also believes that busy or brightly-colored home environments do not help to create a calm, mindful setting, but rather a scattered and stressful one.

You may not see the direct relationship between keeping your kitchen tidy and achieving success with your new marketing business. But in truth, untidiness is associated with low productivity.

Is your home helping to create a good work or rest environment? Here are some tips for implementing orderly and clean habits at home:

1. Sell, donate or give away anything you don't use.

2. Once you've done that, get used to repeating it every six months.

3. Dedicate an hour a day to your house.

4. Have a place for every object.

5. Once you have used it, return each thing to its place.

6. If your home allows it, devote a room to every use, to stop your dining area becoming the place where you eat, rest, study, work out, play with your dog and record videos for social media.

7. Devote a drawer or large box to all the objects you have not yet tidied and which don't have a specific place yet. This will stop them from rattling around your home.

8. Don't accumulate stuff.

9. Create adequate, pleasant and neutral lighting.

10. Only have on your desk things you use every day. Other utensils, documents, and so

on need to go somewhere else. If you're not stapling every day, don't keep a stapler on your desk.

The way we keep our surroundings says something about us. How we commit to the physical (and this goes for our bodies, too) aligns with how we commit to our personal or professional lives. You may be a genius in haute couture or IT, but if you're chaotic with your stuff, it will probably be hard to work with you or be in a relationship with you.

An orderly house also saves you a lot of time, is easier to maintain in financial terms, and favors both rest and concentration. Whatever your goals, taking care of your space should be a transversal and permanent habit.

# Chapter summary

-   Environments, whether physical spaces or communities of people, have a big influence on creating and maintaining your habits.

-   A working, family, friendship or relationship environment that does not let you grow is a toxic one and you need to avoid it.

-   A positive environment, where good habits are underpinned by group strength, is like treasure, and it can drive you more than individual willpower or motivation.

-   A clean and orderly home and workplace has a positive impact on your wellbeing and productivity.

# Analyze your progress

*"The proactive approach to a mistake is to acknowledge it instantly, correct and learn from it."*
— Stephen Covey

Progress rarely occurs evenly; it normally fluctuates, going up and down at various rates. But no matter how small, it is progress if the general trend is upwards.

Since it is irregular, at first it's difficult to see if your new habits have begun to bear fruit. If the changes are small, they can be demotivating because they seem not to be in proportion with the effort you're putting in. The good news is that they multiply exponentially, in such a way that the improvements and rewards will come increasingly faster and be ever greater.

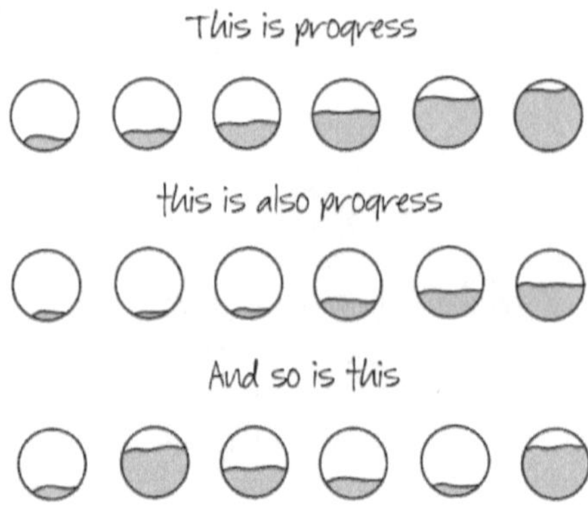


So, if there are not many visible changes at first, why analyze your achievements from day one? Why not wait until things have progressed a little or even until you've reached your goal?

For several reasons. Let's look at a few of them:

1. Getting used to analyzing your progress is another habit that will help you stay focused.

2. You will be more committed to yourself if you know on a regular basis how you're doing.

3. Checking, little by little, that your accomplishments are stacking up will positively reinforce you.

4. Analyzing your progress enables you to detect mistakes or dynamics that you can improve on as soon as possible, so you can anticipate solutions.

5. It will also help you to see how accurate your plan was.

6. Analyzing your progress gives you a general overview of how your plan is going, so you don't get disheartened if you stumble, or kid yourself if it's not going well at all.

7. It will help you in case you go too far and start
   getting obsessed with your goals.

## How to measure your progress

I advise you to analyze your progress without
passing judgement or opinions until you have
looked in depth at what, why and how, being
honest and fair with yourself. Remember that
analyzing your progress isn't about punishing
yourself, but about keeping your feet on the
ground.

Personally, I tend to spend a few minutes each
night assessing how the day went. I also keep a
progress journal where I write down noteworthy
things from each day.

Progress is measured by regularly contrasting
facts, numbers and details.

If you're trying to save money, you should be able to check your new financial habits using figures, budgets, records, and so on, along with the specific and conscious actions you're taking with respect to your money. If you want to lose weight, even though this is annoying at first, you will have to not only weigh yourself but also measure your body fat percentage and muscle mass, the duration and intensity of your workouts, and – no matter how much some quacks will try to convince you of the opposite – you need to track your calories. If you're trying to combat anxiety, you need to be able to check in a journal or log how the process is going, what days have been good or bad, what symptoms you've had, what habits or routines help you, and so on.

If your achievements aren't in line with what you planned, you should adjust and correct. Maybe your plan was too optimistic in terms of time, or maybe too many unexpected things have happened that you couldn't have predicted.

Maybe you relapsed and abandoned your habits more times than you thought.

Measuring your achievements will help you find the key and get you closer to your solution than to disillusionment.

## Learn from others

Another very useful thing for measuring your progress is learning from other people. Why? Because others have already made your mistakes before.

Learning from others is positive because:

- It takes the pressure off: you feel that you're not alone in having to repeat your habits day after day without seeing great results.

- You can spare yourself mistakes that others have shared.

- You can find solutions more quickly if you know about cases similar to yours.

## Sharing information: a habit with a boomerang effect

My patients are often reluctant to share information they found useful. I'm not talking about not telling anyone how much weight they've lost, but maybe sharing that website with diet tips that helped them so much.

If, for example, you've spent a long time trying to improve your personal finances and you're finally starting to do it thanks to new habits you've picked up after reading a new book or have found, after a lot of research, an exceptional money coach, you may be tempted not to tell anyone about something it took you so much effort to discover.

My opinion is that sharing information is a two-way street: if you do it, others will do it for you (not everyone, of course, but that will also help show you who's on your team and who isn't). In addition, life can be unexpected and you don't know what opportunities the future has in store for you. Maybe someone who told someone that you showed them that thing, will have something important for you.

Of course, if you've written a movie script, don't send it to every producer to read – especially if you haven't copyrighted it. If it's good and you haven't covered your back, it will probably be stolen from you. This isn't about working for other people for free. What I *do* think is a good idea is sharing experiences and information with colleagues, even job ads or offers that may be of interest to you: that will transmit the idea that you don't fear rivalry, because you're ready and you believe in yourself.

Sharing your ideas will also give you some feedback on whether they're good or not: of course, you can't please everyone, but if your ideas are rejected by several different people, take a minute to wonder what's up with them.

Another thing: don't be mean. Not with yourself, and not with others. I'm sure that's not who you are.

## A brief note on perfectionism

Are you doing good with the implementation of your new habits? Better than good? Are you following your new habits to a tee and haven't fallen down even once? Are you horrified by the idea of not doing things 100% right?

Then maybe you should listen to what I'm about to say.

I'm glad to hear that you're making so much effort and that your achievements are so impressive week on week. But I must ask you to review your original plan and see if you're on the right path. Because perfectionism has a darker side.

Perfectionism and excellence are not the same thing. Perfectionism is the voice of the oppressor in our heads, and it indicates that our relationships with our habits has become unhealthy and obsessive. While excellence stems from good self-esteem and a willingness to grow, perfectionism is a form of suffering that leads us to value ourselves solely by what we can achieve. Behind excellence is a decision to do what we can and what we need to in order to achieve a goal without forgetting why. Behind perfectionism is self-punishment and fear of failure and rejection.

Having healthy habits also means knowing when to say: "that's enough for today". It's true that it's hard for the habit of going to sleep a half hour earlier to turn into an obsession or addiction, but some habits must be measured in order to avoid pushing your mental health: bigorexia, eating disorders, workaholism or cleaning addiction begin as habits at some point and end up taking the person hostage.

How do you know if you're becoming obsessed?

Good question. There is no infallible formula, but there are clues that can help if you suspect that your habit is getting out of hand:

- If you're spending all day on it: for example, constantly thinking about the calories you've taken in and will be taking in later.

- If the goal and why for that habit seem further and further away from your new life.

- If you're not enjoying the process or are never satisfied.

- If instead of feeling increasingly gratified, performing this routine is bringing you anxiety.

- If you have mood swings, especially in the form of "ups" when you've performed your routine, followed by increasingly long and intense "downs" between one "up" and the next.

- If you lose your cool any time, for any reason, you were unable to stick to your habit, even if it was out of your hands.

- If you feel irritated by people who suggest you take things more slowly.

- If you're doing it in secret or lying so that others leave you alone.

- If it's costing you much more money than you thought it would.

- If it doesn't feel physically or psychologically good for you.

- If it's all you can talk about.

- If you've abandoned your other interests.

- If you think "no one understands" (not even professionals in the field who know more than you do).

- If you're finding it increasingly difficult to maintain a balance between your new habit and your old life, because one is encroaching on the other.

- If you're unable to state your current goal with respect to that habit.

- If you never feel like celebrating your accomplishments.

I recommend that you analyze your progress regularly to detect obsessive behavior. Although one of the early features of an obsession or addiction is lying to yourself, sooner or later you will have to admit to yourself that something's not right.

# Chapter summary

- Analyzing your progress is important to stay focused and make adjustments if necessary.

- It's also a positive reinforcement, especially at the start when progress is small or when your achievements temporarily plateau.

- Making smart comparisons with other people and sharing information are two useful techniques not only for correctly interpreting your progress but also for personal growth.

- I recommend you keep a daily log with details that serve to analyze your progress, and that you spend a few minutes every night reflecting on how you're doing.

- Some habits, like diets or cleaning, for example, can become obsessions. Remember that perfection and excellence are not the same thing.

# Celebrate your achievements

*"Celebration is a confrontation, giving attention to the transcendent meaning of one's actions."*

— Abraham Joshua Heschel

We have all seen an elite sportsperson celebrate their victory in some effusive, ostentatious way: dancing, yelling, thanking God... We, on the other hand, tend not to do that. Can you imagine dancing the samba in front of the courier every time you finish checking your delivery notes? Punching the air triumphantly because you had broccoli for dinner?

But it's so important to celebrate your achievements. Why?

- Celebrating an achievement, triumph or success has a positive impact on your wellbeing and self-esteem, especially if you can immortalize it with a photo (or some other way) so you can remember it at your low points.

- Celebrating an achievement lets other people know about it and generates an opportunity both to receive praise from others and to inspire them with your example, which is highly rewarding.

- Celebrating an achievement strengthens your confidence in the plan and strategy you have adopted.

- Celebrating achievements reinforces your social bonds in a positive way, whether it's at work, in your family, with your partner or with your team.

- Celebrating accomplishments recharges your batteries after the effort you made and prepares you for the next action in a much more positive way than if your achievement went unmarked.

- Celebrating small wins encourages you to aspire to bigger challenges.

Not only should you celebrate your achievements – you also need to celebrate the time you've spent making an effort at something, like your wedding anniversary or a work project.

It's also good to celebrate the achievements of others: you have nothing to be envious about if you, too, are making an effort to better yourself every day (in fact, it's proven that the people who feel the most envy are those who are doing nothing to achieve that goal, while those who are fighting for it and being honest with themselves about their own progress tend not to be jealous of others' progress).

And don't forget to celebrate your birthday, too. Turning a year older and being able to celebrate it with those you love is an achievement in itself and it deserves to be marked and remembered.

How do you celebrate an achievement?

Abraham Joshua Heschel, a leading Jewish theologian, would lament that people nowadays have forgotten the original meaning of celebration. After an achievement, we reward ourselves immediately with a material object or fun activity – when celebrating should actually be a conscious act of reflection on what we achieved and on our gratitude for life. Celebration should be something spiritual, not material. Remember the quotation at the start of this chapter:

"Celebration is a confrontation, giving attention to the transcendent meaning of one's actions."

That said, in my opinion it is also important to treat yourself to something that symbolizes your effort. The way I see it, the most important thing is not to celebrate an achievement by skipping out on your habits, since that has a totally counterproductive message: one of wanting to skip habits that are actually getting you where you want to go.

I recommend that you perform a conscious gratitude exercise and give yourself some quality time to do something you like. Depending on the achievement, this could be trying a new restaurant and different food or even going on a mini-break or treating yourself to a day of totally switching off.

Some ideas:

- Meeting up with loved ones: from a party with friends to a family gathering somewhere fun (remember that there is life beyond family meals – there are endless activities you could enjoy together where you won't end up talking about football or politics).
- An experience.
- A *proper* rest.
- A getaway.
- Buying something related to your habits or goals (from gym accessories to a new tablet for work).

# Chapter summary

- Celebrating your achievements is part of the process of improvement.

- Celebrating your achievements reinforces your self-confidence and your belief in your plan and willpower.

- Celebrating your achievements strengthens your bonds with people around you (family, partner, colleagues, and so on).

- The best way to celebrate an accomplishment is to be aware of the effort involved in it and spend some quality time on yourself.

- You shouldn't celebrate an achievement by skipping out on your habit as a treat, since the message that sends is counterproductive.

## CONCLUSIONS

# Towards constant growth

At the start of this book, we talked about habits as the employees of our lives. We were saying that we want to hire the good ones and fire the bad ones. But I don't just mean defined objectives like losing weight or getting a promotion: this mindset should be a constant in your life, because habits are what make us who we are in every facet of our being.

Don't let a goal by itself define you. Don't abandon yourself because you're already a little better than those around you; aspire to more, explore your own limits, leave a mark on this world. Imagine what you'll think about yourself when you're old.

Although my books are intended to be more of a practical, everyday guide than a philosophical essay on existence, I truly believe that growth should follow growth. That's why you should always make an effort to better your skills and seek growth in yourself, your career and your relationships with others: only the most arrogant athletes stop training when they get ahead, and only athletes who have reduced their potential as people stop taking on challenges after their big sporting victory.

My mission with this book is to add my two cents' worth so that people can find their life purposes and how to reach them. I hope I have managed to do that. And I hope I have conveyed to you the confidence and motivation to live your life better, with more meaning, control and purpose.

If I have, then at the end of these seven steps, all that's left to do is congratulate you.

Because, in truth, your journey began the moment you decided to buy this book and the fact you've come this far means **you've already taken action.** It means you respect yourself and take yourself seriously.

CONGRATULATIONS!

Don't stop now. Never give in, and life will reward you beyond your imagination. It's up to you. Only you have the power to transform your life. Don't put it off till tomorrow. Decide today what your next step will be, and go do it.

The life you want is waiting for you.

Hugs,
Daniel

# Your opinion is very important

As I'm an independent author, your opinion is so important to me and to future readers like you. I would be hugely grateful if you would leave me **a review on your favorite store** to tell me what you thought of my book **so that I can keep on improving it**:

- What did you like best?
- Is there anything you felt was missing
- Who would you recommend it to?
- ...

www.danieljmartin.es/review/poh

# A gift just for you!

Would you like to **read my next book completely FREE?** Scan the code below and **join my readers' club!**

Great surprises await: be the first to read my new releases, listen to my audiobooks for free, get signed and dedicated copies... and much more!

*www.danieljmartin.es/readersclub/*

# Other books by Daniel J. Martin

*http://www.danieljmartin.es/wide/books*

www.ingramcontent.com/pod-product-compliance
Lightning Source LLC
Chambersburg PA
CBHW021003160726
47994CB00006B/2359